superactiv

SKATEBOARDING

James Marsh

Illustrated by David Horwood
Consultant: Andy Horsley

h

Hodder
Children's
Books

a division of Hodder Headline

The information in this book has been thoroughly researched and
checked for accuracy, and safety advice is given where appropriate.
Neither the author nor the publisher can accept any responsibility for any
loss, injury or damage incurred as a result of using this book.

Printed by Clays Ltd, St Ives plc.

Hodder Children's Books
a division of Hodder Headline Limited
338 Euston Road
London NW1 3BH

Meet the author

James Marsh is a freelance writer and author with credits that scroll on into the horizon. You may recognise his name from articles that appear in the *Young Telegraph*, *meg@* and *Big Time*, or from the cover of his two books, *Earth Alert* and *Nature's Wild!*

James is also an actor, working under the stage name James March, and has appeared in lots of British sitcoms and soaps. James has a curious affection for the ukulele (a mystery that needs to be explained), and his claim that he could bore for Britain on the subject of football is irrefutable. In the skateboard stakes, James is no longer a grommet, but he won't be giving up his day job to look for a place in a pro team.

The author would like to thank the following – Judy for her patience; Pete Hellicar and Jon Robson at Unabomber Skateboards for their words of wisdom; Andy Horsley and Wig at 'Sidewalk Surfer' for always being on the end of the phone; David Horwood for his cool illustrations; Kitty Melrose for pulling no punches; editor Lyn Coutts for her hard work; and Anne Clark for the gig.

Introduction

Visit any city anywhere in the world, and you're bound to find a bunch of skaters jumping, sliding and grinding the local terrain as hard as they can. And it doesn't matter where you are or who you are, if you can ride (or almost ride) a board, they'll make you welcome. The skateboard spirit is universal – you've got friends out there you never knew you had!

But how do you ride with style? How do you kickturn, pull ollies and airs? What's the secret to successfully carrying off slick tricks on mini-ramps and verts? And is it really possible to make a career from skateboarding? To find out and to become a member of the coolest club in the world, read on ... and enjoy the ride of your life!

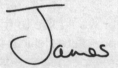

Contents

In the beginning

Wheels, wood and way-haaay!

Did you know that the raddest sport around is just 40 years old? So, why did something as cool as skateboarding take so long to happen? After all, wood for the deck has been around for thousands of years, as has the wheel. So why weren't our prehistoric relatives pulling gnarly tricks at Stonehenge, on Ayers Rock and Table Mountain, or in the Grand Canyon? The answer's easy – they couldn't surf!

This is how it happened. Imagine a gloriously sunny day, beachside in California in the 1950s. Great day in every respect except that the ocean's as flat as a pancake – there's not a wave to be seen – and the would-be-if-they-could-be surfers are mighty bored. The beach dudes are waxing their boards for the umpteenth time when one of them has a moment of genius: "If we nail a rollerskate to a plank of wood, we could ride off down the pavement any time we want." Yo, skateboarding was born!

It took a while to perfect the board's design, and you can be sure those early skaters ate a lot of dirt as they slammed off their boards in crumpled heaps.

*1950s
sidewalk surfer*

*1980s AKT
(after kicktail)*

*1960s BKT
(before kicktail)*

With each tumble, though, came construction and design improvements. Skaters experimented with different shapes and sizes of boards and wheels, and by the late 1960s they were holding competitions with events like high jump, long jump and slalom.

Board talk

If you are not totally familiar with skateboard lingo or can't remember the meaning of a term, look it up in the glossary on pages 115–120.

Hail, the kicktail

The big leap in skateboard design was the kicktail. This is the extra length of board that protrudes behind the rear wheels. When a rider pushes down on the kicktail, the front of the board rises slightly off the ground. This makes the board much easier to steer, and lets you do some radical tricks.

This manoeuvrability gave American skaters the urge to push the sport further. They began to try out moves, both old and experimental, in new skate spots – like water drainage channels, the sloping walls of modern buildings and the bowl-shaped sides of empty swimming pools. These new places demanded new skills and soon skaters were pulling tricks that the first street surfers could only dream of – taking off to achieve massive airs, defying gravity with speeding wallrides, and flipping the board in impossible directions and then landing on it.

The word spread and soon everyone was at it, ripping and shredding the world over. From America and Australia to Europe and Africa, skate parks sprang up and skate meets were organised. Skateboarding had arrived!

But action and slick tricks aren't just confined to skate parks and bowls where skaters are always looking for new lines to ride. The sport has rolled back onto the streets where every kerb, dustbin, gradient and step is an obstacle waiting to be conquered. Today, street skating is how young skaters hone their skills and, more importantly, have fun.

Pro quote

"I just try and have a great time whenever I'm on a skateboard, whether I'm in a competition or not. Skateboarding isn't hard, it's just a matter of letting yourself go."

Bob Burnquist, pro skateboarder

Dressed to thrill

Skate clothing needs to be able to take a beating but still look good. It is also important that the clothes allow you to move freely. For all about safety gear, turn to pages 32–33.

Cap – keeps you cool when things are hotting up. A woollen beanie does the warmth trick in winter and on chilly nights.

T-shirt – designed by skateboard artists. Add to your Christmas list!

Long sleeve shirt – wear unbuttoned over a T-shirt for great looks and to prevent grazing your arms.

Shock-resistant watch – it'll work even when you've slammed tarmac ... again!

Backpack – somewhere to stow your kit when out riding.

Wallet – don't spill your cash if your skating's getting flash.

Canvas belt – to keep your trousers where you want them!

Key-chain – to keep keys safe when pulling gnarly tricks.

Trousers – heavy-weight jeans or combat trousers that are big and baggy.

Trainers – specially designed skate shoes that can take a beating.

Street and vert

Street skating is the style of skating that is done by 99 per cent of skateboarders. You can street skate on the streets and paths around where you live, but you can also do it at your local skate park.

Many street skating moves are based around a jump called the ollie. Once the ollie is conquered, you can tame any obstacle that gets in your way. You can flip your board over bollards, slide on kerbs and grind down handrails. And why do you want to do it? Because it's fun!

Street skating is such an important part of the scene that any competition will have a street skating section. The course will have ramps to speed over, rails to grind and slide, and a fun box. A fun box with its four banked sides topped by a smooth platform is every skater's fave.

The other competition discipline is the vert. Here, skaters pull airs, handstands and slick tricks while speeding up and down a 3.5 to 4.5 metre-high U-shaped ramp. If you want to get enthused about skateboarding, go and watch some pros work their vert routines.

Hey, Grommet!

Don't worry if someone in your skate crew calls you a grommet – they mean no offence. A grommet is someone who is still learning how to skateboard. Don't despair because before long you will be up there nailing gnarly tricks with the best of them.

9

Olden days

In the days before the kicktail, the tricks skaters could pull were limited. Skating was mostly made up of moves that had to be done on slopes found in empty, disused swimming pools or skate parks. Occasionally, someone would organise a slalom competition.

Similar to a skiing race, at slalom skate comps skaters would weave in and out of cones placed in a line. The winner was the one who clocked the fastest time. It was popular for the rush a skater would get travelling at high speed, only just maintaining control of the board.

Another popular form of skating was freestyle. Riders would perform two-minute routines, often to music, including such moves as handstands, board flips and spins.

Freestyle skating sometimes seemed to have more in common with gymnastics or acrobatics than skating. But the tricks that were being used then have now been adapted to create board-moves like kickflips and shove-its – the basic moves of today's street skater.

2 Get on board

Before you can go skating, you need, yes, you've guessed it – a skateboard. There are two types you can buy: professional or ready-made. A professional board is one branded with the name of a professional skater who vouches for the quality and shape of the deck.

A ready-made, off-the-rack board can cost around the same as two CDs, while a pro set-up will set you back five times as much. It's a big difference in price but, as you might expect, the extra cash buys you a better board.

Bargain boards

Many sponsored skaters (find out all about these guys on pages 102–109) have brand new boards that they can sell cheaply.

It's a set up!

A skateboard, also known as a set-up, consists of three main parts: a plywood deck, two trucks and four wheels.

The top of the plywood deck is covered with a sandpaper-like material called griptape. This rough surface makes it easier for the soles of your shoes to grip the board.

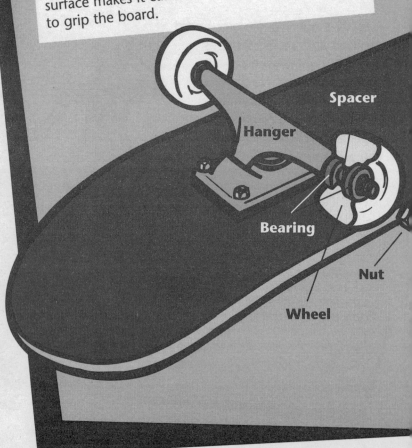

Spacer

Hanger

Bearing

Nut

Wheel

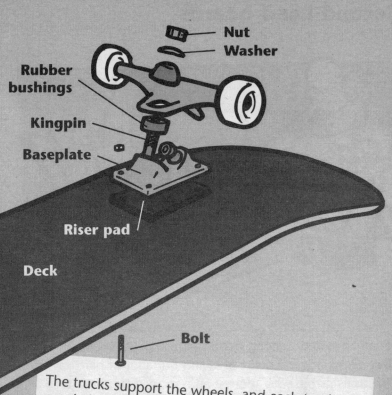

Nut

Washer

Rubber bushings

Kingpin

Baseplate

Riser pad

Deck

Bolt

The trucks support the wheels, and each truck consists of a hanger with an axle inside it, two rubber bushings (to aid steering), a kingpin (to keep the truck stable) and a baseplate. Baseplates fix the trucks to the underside of the deck.

The wheels are held onto the truck by nuts. Bearings with spacers between ensure that each wheel runs smoothly. A riser pad can be placed between the deck and the trucks to give the wheels clearance.

Second-hand boards

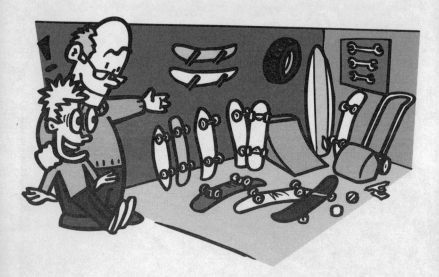

If you're just starting out on your skateboard career, then a ready-made or second-hand board is probably ideal. After all, what's the point of laying out a lot of hard-saved Christmas or birthday money on a souped-up, high-tech pro board when you're not sure if skateboarding is for you.

Pro quote

"When you're just starting out, there's no point buying a flash, mega-expensive board. Get a cheap one and see just how much you like skateboarding. After a couple of months and a dozen sessions at a skate park, you might think, 'Nah, skateboarding's not for me'."

Paul Shier, pro skateboarder

If you're lucky, a friend or relation might have an old skateboard sitting in the garage or loft. Ask around, you'll be amazed at how many old boards have been hidden away just waiting to be used. Alternatively, go along to your nearest skate park and check the noticeboard for 'For sale' notes or simply ask around – there's bound to be someone who wants to sell so they can update.

Even though a second-hand board may be a bit beaten and tattered, it's likely to be of a decent quality (and if it isn't, don't even consider buying it). But before you agree on a price and hand over your precious loot, first give the whole set-up a thorough going-over and then take it for a test-ride. If you're not up to giving it a good road-test, ask someone with a bit of experience to do it for you.

Money matters

It's been estimated that there are over 12 million skateboarders in the world and they're all using the same basic equipment as you – a deck with trucks and wheels. So, don't make the mistake of spending a lot of money on getting the best trucks, the smoothest wheels and the raddest board – if you're still learning, the finest equipment in the cosmos won't make any difference. Save that cash to upgrade your set-up at a later date.

Checking it out

This is what you have to look out for when buying a second-hand board from anyone. A thorough check could save you from having a nasty fall or buying a totally dodgy set-up.

Flat spot will give a bumpy ride

Truck facing the wrong way

Cracked truck

Missing bolt

Wheel of different size and type

Splitting deck (known as "delaminating")

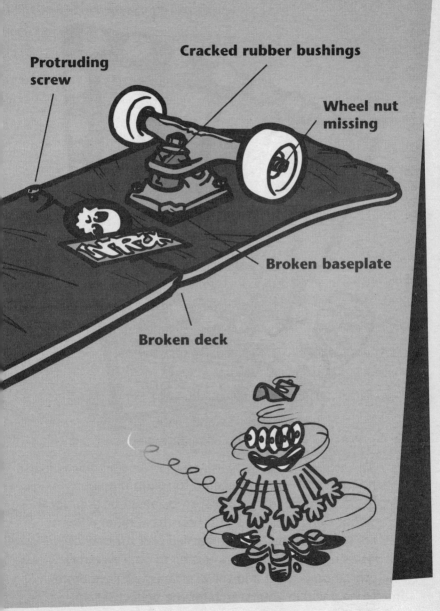

Protruding screw

Cracked rubber bushings

Wheel nut missing

Broken baseplate

Broken deck

Let's talk shop

If you decide that you're prepared to splash out your savings on a pro board, your first stop should be your local skate shop. Like all shops, skate shops have times when they are busy and the staff are hassled and stressed (Saturdays especially). So, if possible, go on a weekday when the shop is quiet and the assistants will have more time to help you in your search for the perfect set-up.

Most skate shops are run by people who love skating, and will therefore do their best to help you. Always remember though that skate shops are not charities, they are in business to make money. And the more of your money they can get, the happier they are.

What this means is that you should always take your time, check out as many skate shops as you can, get feedback on gear from your mates, and think before you buy. For instance, if there's a deck you like – even if it's without wheels – ask if you can stand on it in the shop. See how it feels under your feet. Is it too long? Too wide?

If the owner of the shop won't let you try out the board, note down the name and make of the deck, and then just walk out of the shop. This shop owner doesn't deserve your money, so go and find one that does. And don't worry about getting your hands on that board: you'll find it somewhere else and probably cheaper, too.

Wherever you end up buying your gear, it's a good idea to keep on friendly terms with the staff. You never know when you're going to need their help and advice.

Pro quote

"My first board was a Christmas present from my parents. When I used it, school mates made fun of me. But once I started, I knew that skateboarding was the only thing I wanted to do."
Scott Palmer, skateboarder

Hit the deck!

Assuming your local skate shop isn't run by the shop-keeper from hell, check out the deck. It should be made from six or seven layers of American or Canadian maple that have been glued to together. It will probably be decorated with some cool graphics, though blank boards are available.

The deck will be slightly dish-shaped (this is known as a concave), with the nose and tail curved gently upward. The concave shape makes it easier for you to stay on the deck. The nose of the deck is slightly longer than the tail.

The bottom surface of the deck may have a smooth plastic finish to help the board slide over obstacles. A deck with this plastic facing is called a slick; a deck without the plastic, is known as a wood.

Your final check of the deck should be to ensure that the drillholes for securing the front and back trucks line up with each other. It's a surprisingly common fault, so remember: if they're not in line, the board's not mine. It doesn't take much engineering knowledge to imagine how skew-whiff trucks will affect your ride and control.

Truck stop

Once you're happy with the deck, it's time for the trucks. Made of cast aluminium, these are the gizmos that allow you to steer. Pick one up and you will see that the rubber bushings allow the hanger to twist and turn slightly. This movement gives you steering control and the looser the trucks are, the less effort needed to make a turn.

Get on board

All trucks turn differently, and you may need to try several makes before you find the ones that suit your style. In general though, streamlined and lighter-weight trucks make for faster turns.

Trucks have standard fixing holes, kingpin diameter and axle diameter, so any board or set of wheels can be fitted onto any truck. The only thing you have to worry about is the width of the truck. It should be roughly the same as the width of the deck.

Trucks are the most durable part of a set-up, and if well-maintained will last you a good few years.

Pro quote

"If the trucks don't feel right, it might just be the rubber bushings. Try changing them before you change the trucks – it's much cheaper. Make sure you put the new bushings in the same way as the old ones, though, otherwise the truck will be angled."

Rodney Mullen, pro skateboarder

Truck swap

If your front truck is getting worn through grinding (page 54), swap the trucks around, making sure they face in the same direction as before.

Wheel thing

If you're going to ride, you've got to roll. And to roll you need wheels – four of them. They used to come in just a clay-brown colour, but today they are made in a whole range of colours – from white to lurid shades, such as luminous orange and day-glo purple. So, let's roll with it and check out skateboard wheels.

Wheels are made of a tough, springy plastic called polyurethane and come in a range of sizes and hardness. Smaller wheels with a diameter of 50 to 56 millimetres are light and well-suited to street skating. Wheels with diameters of between 58 to 65 millimetres are heavier and are ideal for skating on rough, cracked concrete. But on the other hand, professional vert skaters often use the large diameter wheels as they make for a faster ride.

When choosing the wheel size, check that when put on the trucks, they don't rub against the deck. If they do, either go for smaller wheels or place a thin, rubber riser pad between the truck and the deck (check out the illustration). The riser pad, or space pad, will lift the board and provide enough clearance for the wheels.

The hardness of polyurethane is given by a durometer reading. Skate wheels are usually given a durometer reading of between 92 and 100. The lower the number, the softer the wheel. Hard wheels are faster and slide more easily, but most street skaters opt for wheels with a 97 to 98 rating.

To ensure a smooth ride and to allow the wheels to run free, you will need two bearings and one spacer per wheel.

Tweaked to suit

Get to know how all the various parts of your set-up work – that way you'll have no trouble adjusting them to suit your personal skating style.

To complete your set-up, a layer of griptape is firmly stuck onto the top of the board. Some shops will give you the griptape free of charge and some won't. If you are buying all your equipment in one shop, you should expect it to be free. Sales assistants may even lay the griptape onto your board as part of their friendly, helpful service!

Once you've chosen your rig, ask if you can watch the assistant put it together. But don't just watch or daydream about grinding and grabs, ask questions. Knowing how each part of the set-up works will make it easier for you to do the maintenance.

Cutting the cost

- Ask at the skate shop if there are any special offers on wheels, trucks, last year's decks, or if there is a discount on buying the whole set-up from their shop.
- Check what the shop throws in for free. Their set-up price might include griptape, labour or stickers. But if you don't make the effort to ask about freebies, the shop assistant is unlikely to tell you.
- Buy a blank, undecorated deck – it's cheaper than one with mega-fancy graphics.
- Get a group of friends together and buy your stuff at the same time. You may get a group discount if you ask.
- Some suppliers set up stands at skate meets and competitions, and sell their equipment at reduced prices.
- Mail order prices are often very competitive but you do have to know exactly what you want. Don't forget to include the cost of the postage in your budget.

Kerbside courtesy

Whenever you're out with your skate crew and find a good spot, don't forget that other people may also be the using the area – and we're not talking about fellow skaters here! If you can keep on the right side of pedestrians by making sure you're not getting in their way unnecessarily, there's less chance you'll be asked to move on.

Try to choose times when your skate spot will be quiet. Going down to the mall on a Saturday morning is just asking for trouble. And try not to have too many bods in your crew – older folks find large numbers of youngsters a bit daunting.

3 | Let's roll

Before racing out to shred the streets with your new board, take a little time to think about where you're going to learn to skate.

It will be a couple of weeks before you become totally familiar with your set-up, and mastered how to start, stop and turn, so until then, a skate park's entrance fee will be a waste of money. The best place to start is somewhere flat, open and uncrowded. A path with grass either side is ideal. Totally avoid any areas with heavy car or people traffic. The car park down the road might look perfect, but it isn't!

Starter's orders

Okay, you're the proud owner of a board and you know you're the coolest thing on the street. Trouble is, you won't look quite so cool when you fall off in front of all your mates. So now it's time to learn the basics of how to start and, more crucially, stop!

First off, are you regular or goofy? What?! Well, just as people are either right- or left-handed, everybody also has a favoured foot. Stand on the board with your right foot as your back foot, then change round so that your left is at the back. Which position (stance) feels the most natural and comfortable?

GOOFY   REGULAR

If the back foot is your right foot, you're regular-footed. Whereas, if that back foot is your left ... yes, you've guessed it – hi there, goofy-foot.

Being regular or goofy makes no difference to how you skate. All the diagrams in this book show regular-footed skaters, so goofy-footed skaters do as exactly as shown but with your feet in opposite positions.

Taking a stance

The hippest thing in skating is the switch stance. This means that you can successfully pull off tricks in both regular and goofy positions. Start off learning tricks by alternating between the two positions and you'll be way ahead of the pack.

Striking the pose

Some beginners fall off their newly-acquired boards because they keep their legs too rigid. Try to think of your legs as shock absorbers – if they're bent, they can take any unexpected bumps.

The top half of your body should be relaxed, with your arms dangling freely by your sides. Think cool and chilled out, and your skating stance will be just right! Even when using your arms for balance, don't stick them out so they're stiff and rigid. You're not walking a tight-rope across Niagara Falls, you're hanging loose on your board.

The first step

STEP 1
Find a flat area where you can hold onto a wall. Make sure the board is stationary, then put your front foot at a slight angle onto the board just behind the front truck.

STEP 2
Keep your weight on your back foot. Gently push off with your back foot and swing it smoothly onto the board and position it just over the back truck.

STEP 3
Swivel your feet so they are parallel and pointing across the deck. Now you're on your way! Keep a loose stance with your legs and knees relaxed. Use your arms for balance.

Front foot first

Never put your back foot on the board before your front foot – the board will shoot out from under your feet like a racing car.

Woaaahh!

There are two safe ways of stopping. The first is to take your back foot off the tail of the board and slide it along the ground until you come to a halt. The second is more difficult, but saves wear and tear on the soles on your trainers plus you will stop in double-quick time.

Here's how to do the trainer-saving stop – take your back foot off the board, but instead of dragging it along the ground, you do a one-legged run keeping the front foot on the board.

Now you can stop and start. Who said skateboarding was difficult, huh?

Getting your balance

To practise getting your balance, place the board on grass or carpet and then stand on the board. Grass or carpet will stop the board flying off unexpectedly, and give you somewhere soft to land!

Play safe

Skaters need to protect the most vulnerable parts of their bodies – the head, knees, elbows, wrists and hands. And that means wearing a helmet, knee pads, elbow pads, and wrist guards or gloves.

Helmet – this should be padded and made of light plastic. It should fit snugly without being tight and uncomfortable. If your helmet is too big, it will simply fall off.

Wrist guards – dead useful when skating on any sort of ramp. Hard plastic splints inside the wrist guards prevent the wrists being bent into positions nature never intended.

Gloves – use these to protect hands from grazes and cuts. You don't have to buy special skating gloves – a pair of thick, leather, gardening or builders' gloves will do just as well.

Knee pads and elbow pads – these are essential for protection and to absorb shock. The skating careers of several pros have been cut short simply because of damage to unprotected knees.

Fall guys

When you're learning to skate or trying new tricks, you're bound to hit the deck occasionally. To make these tumbles as painless as possible and injury-free, always wear protective gear and learn the techniques of bailing.

Pro quote

"If you learn to skate wearing protective gear, it will give you extra confidence – because you know that when you fall, your joints are covered."
Peter Hellicar

Bailing 1

STEP 1
Use this bail when you feel you've lost control and can't land safely on your feet. Place the board on grass and stand on it. Crouch low and try to remain relaxed.

STEP 2
Roll sideways onto the ground, falling onto as much of your body as possible. Don't tense your body or put your hands out to break your fall. Use your arms to protect your head.

Bailing 2

This technique will lessen the momentum of your fall and ensure that your hips and bottom are the first to hit the turf.

When you start to fall, crouch low and push yourself backwards off the board with your legs. When your rear hits the ground you can roll over as shown in step 2 on page 34 to lose more speed. Keep your hands and arms in front of your body or to the sides.

Skate fact

The longest distance ever travelled on a skateboard is 436.6 kilometres (271.1 miles). This super-skating feat took place in Greece and was accomplished by Eleftherior Argiropoulos after one and a half days of non-stop rolling.

Turn for the better

Steering on a skateboard couldn't be simpler – all you have to do is lean.

BACKSIDE TURN
Get the board moving forward and then, keeping your knees and hips slightly bent, lean forward and press down with your toes. The board will turn in the direction your toes are pointing. Use your arms to help you keep balance.

FRONTSIDE TURN
To turn the opposite way or frontside, simply lean backwards and press your heels onto the edge of the board. The more you lean, the tighter the turn. Use your arms for balance.

Turn control

If you find it difficult to control your turns, tighten the trucks' kingpins so that there isn't so much give. As your turns improve, loosen the kingpins by half a turn a day.

Weather warning

Never ride in the rain. The water will soak into the deck causing the plywood to split, it will get into the bearings and seize them up, and any steel components will start to rust.

First service

Check your set-up each time you go skating. If you are unsure about what to do, your local skate shop will show you how it's done for a small charge.

- Spin the wheels to check they are running smoothly. If they wobble, carefully tighten the wheel nuts with a skateboard wrench.
- Wipe the bearings with a cloth. Don't oil them – they are pre-greased and you will only make them dirty.
- To even the wear on wheels, swap each one with the wheel diagonally opposite.
- Replace rubber bushings that have started to split.
- Check that the trucks are secure. If they are loose, gently tighten the bolts. Be careful not to overtighten or you will pull the bolts through the deck.
- Replace worn or peeling griptape.
- Smooth minor cracks and splits on the deck with sandpaper. Bad cracks running across or down the length of the board, may mean it's time to splash out and buy a new deck.

First aid

Sometime during your skateboarding career, either you or a member of your crew is sure to suffer an injury. Most skate injuries are confined to bruises, grazes, cuts, sprains and dented egos, but there's a right way and a wrong way of treating even the most minor of scrapes.

If the injured skater appears to be in severe pain, tell them to stay where they are, keep them warm, and phone for an ambulance.

BRUISES
Make a cold compress from a clean tissue or towel by soaking it in cold water and squeezing out excess water. If you're skating the streets away from home, you can always find clean water in the rest rooms of garages and fast food restaurants. Hold the compress against the bruise to reduce swelling and pain. Keep the compress clean and moist.

GRAZES
Wash the wound gently with a clean cloth and plenty of clean water to remove any dirt. If it's a really nasty graze, go to a hospital.

CUTS
Press a cold, clean compress firmly onto the cut. If you can raise the cut area into the air, it will help to stem the bleeding. If the wound is bleeding heavily, maintain the pressure on the compress and head to the nearest hospital.

SPRAINS
Apply a cold compress to reduce pain and swelling. If the sprain is serious, it may conceal a broken bone. If in doubt, go to hospital.

Better safe than sorry

Head injuries can be very
dangerous. If a fellow skater
suffers a bad fall and bangs
their head, always make
sure they go to a hospital
to be checked out.
There may not be any
visible sign of injury,
and your friend may
insist that they feel
okay but you'll be
doing them a real
favour if you cart them
off to the nearest
casualty department.
If the skater is sick or
complains of blurred
vision or a stinking
headache, get them
to hospital as
quickly as possible.

Kit bits

*It's a good idea to have a small first aid kit in your
backpack. All you need are: large, strong sticking
plasters; antiseptic wipes and cream; a clean cloth;
and a tube of sun protection cream.*

Golden rules

- Always wear safety gear.
- Warm up before you start skating – stretching exercises really help.
- Learn to fall properly.
- Don't try a new trick until you feel you are ready.
- If you are injured, stop skating immediately and tend to your injury.
- If someone has to go to hospital, go along with them to offer support. That's what friends are for.
- If you are coming back from injury, be sure that it has fully healed before you get back on your board. Consider wearing a support bandage on the injured area until it's back to full strength.

4 Getting tricky

Now that you're comfortable with starting, stopping and turning your board, it's time to learn some gnarly moves. Many of these moves use that wonderful invention at the back of your board, the kicktail. The first move that uses the kicktail is the kickturn, and it's a good idea to practise kickturns in a stationary position, in both directions. Then when you're confident, try using them to change direction at slow speeds.

Park life

Once you've mastered the basics and you're feeling confident, head to your local skate park. Watch the other skaters practise their moves, and take special notice of the lines they take. Some parks have instructors who will help you find your way around and show you new moves.

Kickturn

STEP 1

Move your front foot to the
middle of the board, and
your back foot onto the
kicktail. Press lightly down
on the kicktail with your back
foot. The front wheels will lift
slightly off the ground.

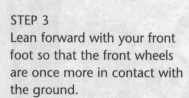

STEP 2

Twist your body 45 degrees
in the direction your heels are
facing. The board will follow
and move in that direction.

STEP 3

Lean forward with your front
foot so that the front wheels
are once more in contact with
the ground.

Customising

*Customise your board by putting stickers on the
bottom of the deck. Skate shops sell them cheaply,
and some manufacturers send them out for free.*

Tic-tac and 360

A combination of kickturns, first in one direction and then the other, is known as a tic-tac. The tic-tac will also increase the speed of the board.

To do a 360, simply follow steps 1 and 2 of the kickturn but instead of twisting only 45 degrees, twist your upper body quickly through a full circle (360 degrees). The board, spinning on the back wheels, should follow, and both you and the board will turn a full circle.

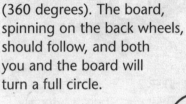

180 frontside slide

To slow down without putting your feet on the ground, you can do a 180 frontside slide (the instructions are on the next page). Slides are great for taking some speed out of a run, look dramatic and make a great noise. Try not to do them too near to unsuspecting passers-by – they may not appreciate the shock!

180 frontside slide

STEP 1
As you move forward at a medium speed, lean back slightly towards your heels and press down gently on the nose. Use your arms to keep your balance throughout this move.

STEP 2
Twist your shoulders to face forwards and, keeping your weight on the front truck, use your back foot to push the board round. The back wheels will slide round while the front ones remain almost stationary.

STEP 3
Once the board has rotated 180 degrees around the nose, it should come to a halt. The flashy 180 frontside slide is easier than you thought!

Faking it!

If, after doing that 180 frontside slide, you carried on moving in the same direction but facing the opposite way, you've pulled a fakie manoeuvre! A fakie is travelling backwards at any point during a move and may be as simple as riding up a little incline and then just rolling back down again. This easy move is called rolling down to fakie.

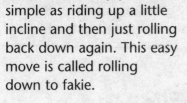

Pull a wheelie

When you lean on the kicktail to make the nose rise while moving forward, you've done a manual or wheelie. You can also do a nose wheelie (check out the illustration right) by gently pressing down on the nose with your front foot. The nose mustn't touch the ground. If it does, you'll be eating dirt! Working out just how much pressure to apply, simply takes practice.

Air apparent

Not all skateboarding takes place on the ground, many moves are carried out in the air. The basis for most of those tricks is the ollie. Made famous by Allen "Ollie" Gelfand in the mid to late 1970s, this slick trick allows you to leap into the air with the board seemingly glued to your feet. But before, trying an ollie, it's worth getting used to the feeling of air beneath your board.

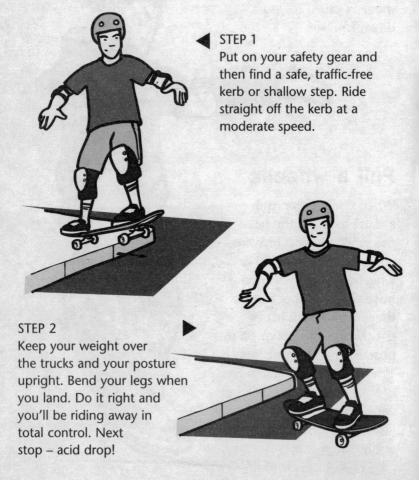

◀ STEP 1
Put on your safety gear and then find a safe, traffic-free kerb or shallow step. Ride straight off the kerb at a moderate speed.

STEP 2
Keep your weight over the trucks and your posture upright. Bend your legs when you land. Do it right and you'll be riding away in total control. Next stop – acid drop!

Acid drop

Keep practising until your take-off and landing are seamless, then try finding slightly higher drops. As you increase the height of this trick, it becomes an acid drop. There's no saying what that height is – but you'll know when you've done it.

Skaters say that the take-off is easier if you do a slight wheelie (page 45) as you come up to the edge of drop.

Shoe-per glue

If your trainers are starting to feel the effects of some hard skating, fill any holes in the soles with silicone rubber shoe repair glue. You can get it from shoe repair shops and some skate shops and it's cheaper than a new pair of trainers. The repair won't last forever but it'll keep you grinding and sliding for a while longer.

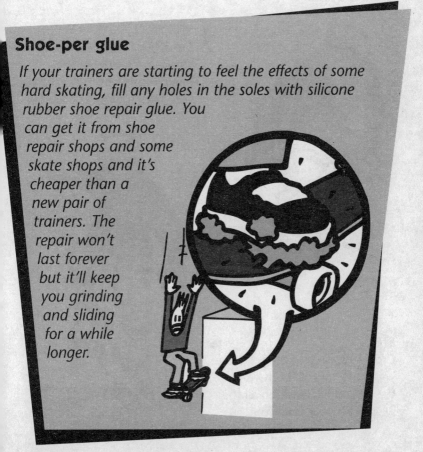

Ollie patch

The importance of the ollie to skateboarding cannot be over-emphasised, it is the key to just about everything you're ever going to do on your skateboard. No matter how long it takes you to perfect the ollie, it will be worth it – so hang on in there.

Start by doing an ollie in a stationary position, and only when you're comfortable with the move should you try it while moving.

STEP 1
Move your front foot about 7 centimetres (3 inches) behind the front truck. Leave your back foot on the kicktail.

STEP 2
Crouch down and then slap your back foot down hard on the kicktail while taking all the weight off your front foot.

STEP 3
As the board starts to rise vertically, drag your front foot towards the nose. At the same time, bring your back foot up into a jumping position.

STEP 4
With your front foot at the nose, control the board so that it levels out in mid-air.

STEP 5
Land with your feet firmly planted as shown in the illustration right.

Kickflip

This is very similar to an ollie except that you are spinning your board in mid-air. Don't worry about the height of your kickflip to begin with, it's nailing down the technique that counts. The move may sound tricky, but all it takes is practise and patience.

Pro quote

"It's just the flicking of your toes on the heel edge that makes the board spin around. Otherwise, it's just like any other ollie."

Kareem Campbell, pro skateboarder

STEP 1
Follow steps 1 and 2 of the ollie (pages 48–49), but place your front foot slightly closer to the heel edge.

STEP 2

Pop the board with your back foot, then flick the heel edge of the board with the toes of your front foot to make the board spin.

STEP 3

Once the board has spun right around, 'catch' the board with your feet and get ready to land. Absorb the landing shock by having your knees bent. Keep your balance by extending your arms.

Pro quote

"Skateboarding's not about who's number one. It's about having fun."

Justin Watene, skateboarder

Oi! No skateboarding!

Some adults think that skateboarders are just vandals on wheels, and this means that security guards, police or householders may hassle you to move on. If this happens, you must be polite. A friendly attitude on your part may change the whole situation. One thing's for sure, if you're rude, give verbal or get stroppy, then you're bound to be given marching orders. A bad attitude could also mean that you've ruined that particular skating spot for everyone else.

The best thing to remember is: never skate too long in one area – keep moving!

If you're skating on private property, then pack up quick – you're trespassing. If you're riding public areas, then you may well be within your rights to be there. But there's no point aggravating a situation that could be handled in a much more diplomatic way. Following are some situations that you may have to face.

Hassled by a security guard – politely ask who you (or your parents) can contact about getting permission to skate in that area. If there's no joy, then ask if it is okay to skate in a nearby area. Still no luck? Then get rolling.

Police tell you to skate elsewhere – don't argue, just do as they say. Many councils have introduced special by-laws banning skating in certain areas, or imposed on-the-spot fines. But before you shoot off, ask the police if they know where you can skate legally.

Householder asks you to move – politely ask if there is a reason. If you can relieve their worries, terrific, but if not then it's push-off time. Report it to your parents who may be able to sort it.

Serious hassle

If you are ever threatened – verbally or physically – or if someone tries to physically move you from an area, tell your parents. They can follow it up to ensure that it doesn't happen again. Don't hang around to make a bad situation worse.

5 Radical moves

Life's a grind if you're a skateboarder. But for skateboarders that's just fine, because a grind – dragging the board's metal trucks along an edge – is one of the raddest, coolest moves around.

Pro quote

"Grinds are what dreams are made of – blocks, bars and rails weren't made to keep people off the grass, they were really made to grind!"

Brian Sumner, skateboarder

So, how do you grind? First, you'll need to be confident of being able to ollie onto the edge of an object whilst remaining in control – a move called an ollie to axle – then you can progress to doing metal mentals with a 50-50.

Ollie to axles

Approach a kerb head-on, ollie up to it and twist through 90 degrees so that the board lands on the kerb on its trucks. Remain stationary on the kerb before flipping the board off.

50-50

STEP 1
Approach parallel to a kerb or low metal coping (that's the metal piping that runs along the edge of ramps) at a moderate speed.

STEP 2
Ollie onto it and land in the ollie to axle position. The trucks will drag along the edge.

STEP 3
Before you lose too much speed, push down on the kicktail with your back foot and steer off the edge. So, are you the grind king or what?!

Radical moves

When you've landed a few successful 50-50s, try to see if you can make a 5-0. Approach the kerb as you would for the 50-50, ollie onto the edge but land on just the back truck and grind along with the nose pointing upwards in a manual (page 45). When you start to lose speed, steer the board off the kerb and land.

So far, all these grinds have been backside (it helps to remember the *back* faces the out*side* of the move) – now try to see if you can pull them off frontside as shown right. At the same time, try to make your grinds as phat (said 'fat') as possible – that's really long or really fast.

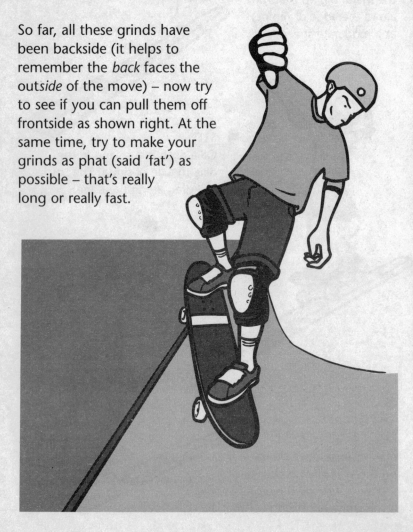

Grind on

A variation of the 5-0 is the Smithgrind. Here, you land on your rear tuck but with the nose of your deck hanging off the front of the kerb. The deck can touch the edge of the kerb but it's cooler if it doesn't.

A really popular grind is the crooked or k-grind. This is when you grind with the front truck whilst keeping the back truck in the air. You'll need to be moving a little faster than before and it takes a lot of control. Too much pressure from your front foot and the board will come to a sudden stop whilst you continue to move forward. Hey presto, it'll be slam time!

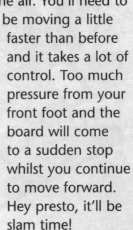

Wickedly sick

If someone says the move you've pulled is 'sick', don't worry – it means they think you've just done something really, really good!

Who are you calling feeble?

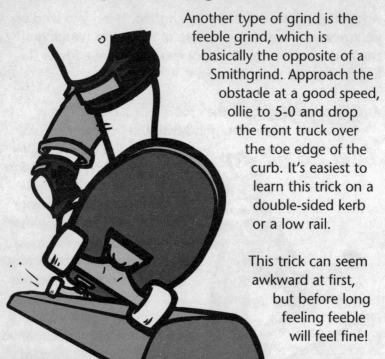

Another type of grind is the feeble grind, which is basically the opposite of a Smithgrind. Approach the obstacle at a good speed, ollie to 5-0 and drop the front truck over the toe edge of the curb. It's easiest to learn this trick on a double-sided kerb or a low rail.

This trick can seem awkward at first, but before long feeling feeble will feel fine!

Slap happy

You don't have to ollie into a grind if it's a low kerb, you can pull a slappy instead. To do a slappy, approach the kerb you want to grind, and just ease the pressure off your front foot to let the front truck rise onto the kerb. Then, put the weight back onto your front foot, ease your back truck onto the kerb and get grinding.

Slippery tip

Skaters often rub blocks of wax (usually candle wax) up and down kerbs and rails to make them more slippery for grinds and slides.

Ollies to go, go, go

To keep on adding to your repertoire of tricks, it's crucial to have a whole heap of moves under your belt. These ones combine ollies, kickturns, grinds and more!

First up, is the 180 ollie – a move that puts together an ollie (pages 48–49) and a kickturn (page 42). This is how it goes: ollie up then swivel your upper body, and allow your lower body and the board to follow until your back foot becomes the leading foot.

To finish, land and then either ride out fakie (page 45), or pull a quick 180 kickturn so that your front foot is leading once more. As with other tricks, this move can be completed backside and frontside – practise both.

Who nose?

It's possible to do an ollie from the nose of the board, by popping the nose rather than the tail. This trick, called a nollie (instructions are on the next page), takes a lot of patience and bails to learn. It's best to practise the nollie in a stationary position.

Nollie

STEP 1
Slide your front foot to the nose of the board, and move your back foot to the middle. The back foot takes most of the weight.

STEP 2
Crouch down and then push down hard with your front foot while releasing the weight from your back foot.

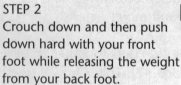

STEP 3
As the board rises, let your back foot bring the board up level. To land, position your feet over the trucks.

The snag of the moving nollie is making sure that when you pop the nose, it doesn't bring you to a standstill. Once you've nailed a nollie, combine it with a kickflip or, if you're really confident, a heelflip (page 61).

Heelflip

A heelflip spins the board like a kickflip but uses the heel of your front foot to do the flipping. The heelflip, ollie and kickflip are the core of street skating. Visit any park, and you'll see skaters mixing flips with other moves to create an endless repertoire of new tricks.

To do a heelflip, start as if you're doing a regular ollie then as the board begins to level out in the air, drag your front foot towards the toe edge. Do this by moving your toes then the ball of your foot and, finally, your heel. The board will flip – catch it with your feet, land and ride away.

Shove-it

You can also combine an ollie with a shove-it to create a pop shove-it. But first you need to learn the shove-it. In a shove-it, the board turns through 180 degrees while you're in the air above it.

STEP 1
Keep your weight on the back foot and place your front foot over the nose. Press down with your front foot so the tail rises.

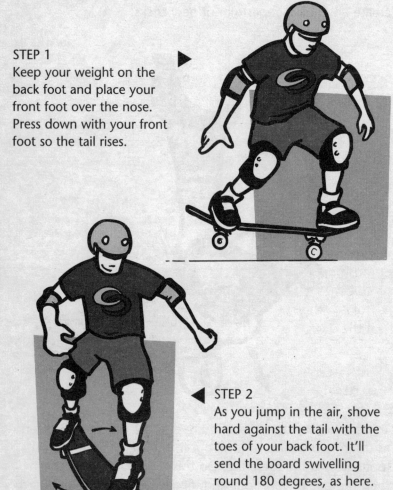

STEP 2
As you jump in the air, shove hard against the tail with the toes of your back foot. It'll send the board swivelling round 180 degrees, as here.

STEP 3
Land back on the
board, with the tail
facing forwards.

Backside pop shove-it

To make a backside pop shove-it, put your front foot in the
ollie position and your back foot in the centre of the tail. As
you push down on the tail, flick out your back foot behind
you to turn the board. Let the board rotate 180 degrees,
control it with your front foot and land. To go frontside,
pitch the deck in the opposite direction.

Pro quote

*"The pop shove-it is a back foot trick, you don't really
use your front foot at all. Don't put your back foot
all the way to the end of the tail or it will make
the board flip over."*
Josh Friedberg, pro skateboarder

6 Park and ride

Skill centre

If you haven't already done so, it's time to get you and your stick down the skate park to meet some like-minded people who can do tricks you've never even dreamt about.

Every park is different, but most will have a ramp and a few obstacles with metal coping for grinds.

Skate parks also vary in what they charge in entrance fees. Some skate parks are run by the local council or a similar authority and are free (yes!), others will make a small charge to let you through the gate (uh-huh), while there are those that are commercially-run operations wanting proper cash (boo!). It all depends on where you live.

Skate park goodies

It's unlikely that a single park will have all of the following but visit enough parks, and in time you'll get to see (and ride) them all.

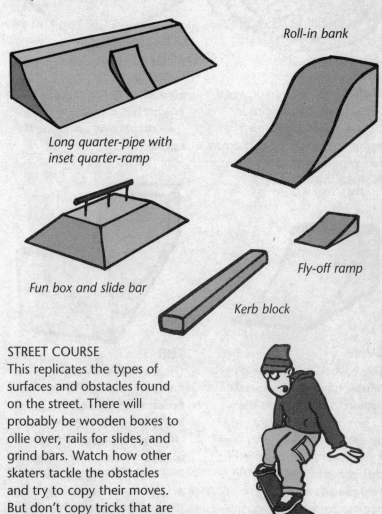

Roll-in bank

Long quarter-pipe with inset quarter-ramp

Fun box and slide bar

Fly-off ramp

Kerb block

STREET COURSE
This replicates the types of surfaces and obstacles found on the street. There will probably be wooden boxes to ollie over, rails for slides, and grind bars. Watch how other skaters tackle the obstacles and try to copy their moves. But don't copy tricks that are still well beyond your ability.

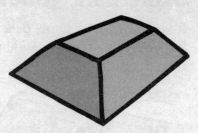

BOWL
Made from concrete or wood, bowls have their origins in curved-walled Californian swimming pools. Long, narrow and wiggly bowls are known as snake runs.

FUN BOX
Four small ramps placed against a low platform make the competition favourite, the fun box.

RAMPS
These wooden, quarter-pipe ramps, topped with metal coping, curve up into the air to give skaters an extra dimension to their sport. The most popular are mini-ramps that come in different sizes. Two ramps can be put back-to-back so that skaters can jump over the spine.

VERT
Originally known as the half-pipe, the vert is the most taxing form of skating. Usually made of wood, these giant U-shapes are up to 3.5 to 4 metres (11 to 12 feet) high. Pros will throw massive airs and pull spinning twists; other skaters just enjoy the thrill of riding them.

Snake in the grass

*Don't get a reputation for being a snake. A snake is
someone who jumps the queue for the goodies
at skate parks.*

Slippin' and slidin'

It's not just the wheels and trucks that can be used for
moves. Skaters also perform tricks called slides which use
the middle and ends of their decks.

STEP 1
To get used to the feeling of landing
on the middle of your board,
approach a low two-sided kerb and
ollie onto it so that the board straddles
the kerb at right angles. Make sure
your legs remain bent and that you
use your arms to keep your balance.

STEP 2
Look over your trailing shoulder to twist
your body, and jump off the kerb. This
last move is important because when
you finish a rail slide, unless you
turn your board through
90 degrees, you will land
sideways rather than with
the nose pointing forwards.

Park and ride

STEP 3 ▶

When you're happy with the action, approach a low rail at a slight angle and ollie onto it so that you land on the centre of your board, towards the end of the rail. Your momentum will slide you to the end, where you have to turn the board to land with the nose forward.

Gradually build up the speed at which you approach the rail and increase the distance you travel along it. Before you know it, you'll be sliding the entire length of the rail.

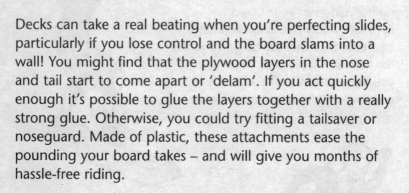

Decks can take a real beating when you're perfecting slides, particularly if you lose control and the board slams into a wall! You might find that the plywood layers in the nose and tail start to come apart or 'delam'. If you act quickly enough it's possible to glue the layers together with a really strong glue. Otherwise, you could try fitting a tailsaver or noseguard. Made of plastic, these attachments ease the pounding your board takes – and will give you months of hassle-free riding.

Queue here

Skate parks have busy times when you'll end up queuing more than skating. Don't waste precious riding time – go back when it's quiet.

Pro quote

"The best way to learn tricks is in your head. Before I go to sleep I think about tricks. If I haven't been able to do something, I go home and think about it. Sixty per cent of skateboarding is in your head; the rest is your legs."

Rob Selley, pro skateboarder

Jump!

You and your crew will invent all sorts of crazy moves and sketchy tricks. One trick that has been popular since the 1970s is the high jump.

To make a jump, lay a thin strip of wood across two stacks of bricks. Ride your board up to it, leap over the wood while your deck goes under and then land back on your deck. The challenge is to see how high you can jump. Trevor Baxter's world record for this stands at 1.67 metres (63 inches)!

Nose slide

▶

STEP 1
Approach a kerb so that you're riding almost parallel to it.

▶

STEP 2
Do a half 180 ollie so that the board lands at right angles to the kerb with the front truck pressing against the edge of the kerb.

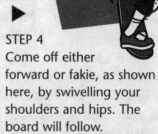

▶

STEP 3
Place most of your weight on the front foot to control the slide.

STEP 4
Come off either forward or fakie, as shown here, by swivelling your shoulders and hips. The board will follow.

To do a tail slide follow the same method, but make the ollie higher in order to get the tail onto the kerb.

7 On the up

Pump it!

Any skater
planning to
attack a bowl
or mini-ramp
must be able
to pump.
Pumping is the
technique used
by skaters so
that they can
travel higher
and higher
up the steeply,
curved walls.

Before you try
pumping, have a
good look at the
bowl or ramp. It's well worth just taking a walk along it.
The points where the horizontal areas start to curve
upwards are known as transitions or trannies.

Geared up for safety

*Never skate bowls or ramps without wearing a helmet,
elbow pads, knee pads and gloves.*

Warming up!

To get to grips with a bowl or ramp, ride your board along the bottom, gently riding up the lower part of the transition. You'll have to lean and shift your weight to accommodate the slope. Then try gently rolling straight up the transition and, when the board slows and stops, let yourself roll down fakie.

Pumping station

Now for pumping. As you approach the trannie, throw your upper body forward to increase your speed. Then, as you start to slow and roll backwards, crouch down. As you roll past the trannie, stand up again. It's a bit like being on a swing – you slowly increase your speed by using your body's weight. Going forwards is easy, it's going backwards that needs practice!

Speedy skate fact

So you think you're fast up the ramp. Have you ever heard of Roger Hickey? No, well listen up. Roger has clocked 89 kilometres (55 miles) per hour standing on a skateboard, and hit over 126 kilometres (78 miles) per hour lying down. But it's not only records he's broken – Roger has sustained 44 fractures in his pursuit of speed!

Having a bail

Skating transitions can be dangerous if you're not sure how to bail correctly. This is how experienced skaters fall without hurting themselves.

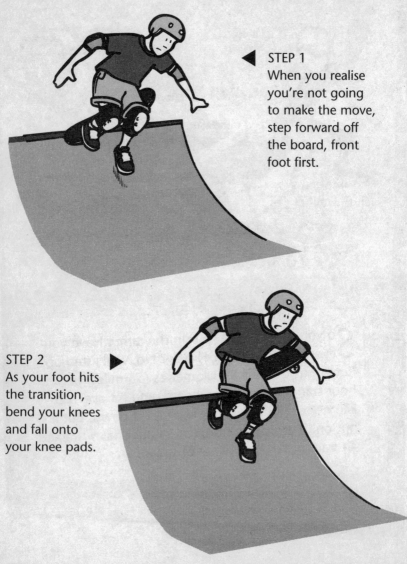

STEP 1
When you realise you're not going to make the move, step forward off the board, front foot first.

STEP 2
As your foot hits the transition, bend your knees and fall onto your knee pads.

STEP 3
Slide down the ramp or bowl on your knee pads and the tops of your shoes.

STEP 4
Reach the end of the trannie safely and ... smile!

If you're still a bit stressed about how it's done, ask – there's always someone working or watching the ramp who'll be happy to show you.

Pro quote

"As you get better at riding mini-ramps, increase your speed and start travelling across the ramp. That way, when you hit the coping at an angle, you can introduce slides and grinds."

Brad Hayes, pro skateboarder

Getting lippy

As you get to know the feeling of riding the transitions and become used to going higher, you'll want to add in the tricks learned on the flat. A good one to start with is the 180 kickturn.

Before you reach the lip of the ramp or bowl, press down with your back foot and spin the board round to head off forward down the slope. When doing this, always make sure you're facing sideways across your board.

Do drop in

You don't have to begin every ramp trick by starting at the bottom. You can start from the top by dropping in. Don't worry that it doesn't seem right (or even sensible) to launch yourself off a steep slope – just imagine the thrill when you do it!

STEP 1
Stand at the top of the ramp and place your board with the back truck pressing against the coping. Put your back foot firmly on the tail to hold the board in position.

◀ STEP 2
Put your front foot over the front truck, but leave your weight on the back truck. Keep your knees bent and legs flexible.

STEP 3 ▶
Lean forward onto your front foot, push your wheels down the slope and ride away. If you think you're going to fall, use the bail technique shown on pages 74–75.

Pro quote

"Some people find it easier to drop in if they hold the nose of the board with their leading hand."

Neal Hendrix, pro skateboarder

Lip service

The first liptrick to add to your range of moves is the axle stall. It's very similar to the ollie to axle you learned in chapter 5.

STEP 1 ▶

Ride straight up the ramp towards the lip. Just before you hit the coping, start a 90 degree backside kickturn while pushing down on the tail to raise the front wheels.

▲
STEP 2
As your back truck hits the coping, turn your upper body through 90 degrees, letting your legs and board follow.

▲
STEP 3
Push your front truck onto the coping, hold the position for a few seconds before turning back down the slope.

Let's rock and roll

No, it's not time to hit the dance floor, a rock 'n' roll is another liptrick. During this move, the deck will rock on the coping, before you roll off down the transition.

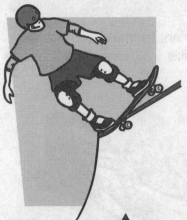

STEP 1
Ride straight up the ramp towards the lip. Just before you hit the coping, press down on the tail to lift the front wheels over the lip.

STEP 2
Let the deck rest in the 'rock' position – front wheels on top of the ramp, middle of the deck on the coping and back wheels touching the top of the vertical. Use your arms to keep your balance.

STEP 3
After a second or so, press down on the tail to lift the nose and do a 180 kickturn so that you roll forwards down the ramp.

Rock fakie

A variation of the rock 'n' roll is the rock fakie. Follow steps 1 and 2 of the rock 'n' roll, but instead of rolling the board round with a kickturn, just lift the nose so that you ride fakie back down the transition.

During this variation, it's important to make sure that you lean back as you start rolling fakie – otherwise you'll end up bailing fakie!

It's a disaster

When your rear wheels are on top of an object, the deck on the edge of it, and the nose hanging off, it's a disaster. No, really, that's its name – a disaster.

Fakie tail stall

To nail a fakie tail stall, ride your board backwards up the slope, and as you reach the coping, push down on the tail so that it rests on top of the coping. The back wheels will be pressing against the coping.

Not only do you need to time the placing of the tail, you also need to have enough speed to reach the top without overshooting. It's a difficult trick that takes patience to perfect, but so cool and controlled once you get it.

8 Up for grabs

All hands on deck

Up until now, your moves have been all to do with your feet – now it's time to get your mitts busy. Lots of moves can be combined with grabs to create totally new tricks. From a basic blunt-and-grab to the stylish ollie stalefish these tricks are guaranteed to grab attention!

Skate fact

The greatest distance jumped from one skateboard to another is 5.8 metres (19 feet) by 1980s skate star Tony Alva. He cleared 17 barrels before landing on the second skateboard that had been placed at the end of the jump.

Basic blunt

STEP 1
Pump up and down the transition on a gentle mini-ramp until you have enough speed to reach the coping. Roll straight up the transition towards the lip.

STEP 2
When the back wheels roll over the coping, press down on the tail to stop the board. The back wheels should rest on the coping while the nose is pointing up in a near vertical position.

STEP 3
Grab the rail (or edge) of the board between the trucks with your leading hand. Hop backwards by pushing with your back leg and pulling with your arm, then roll fakie back down the ramp.

Taking the air

The ollie grab to fakie is like a blunt but instead of balancing the board on the coping, you ollie at the top of the ramp, execute your grab and then roll down fakie. Are you ready?

STEP 1
Aim your board straight up the ramp with your front foot towards the middle of the board. At the top of the ramp get ready to ollie.

STEP 2
Push down the tail and slide your front foot forward. Don't forget that because of the trannie, your ollie will be nearly vertical.

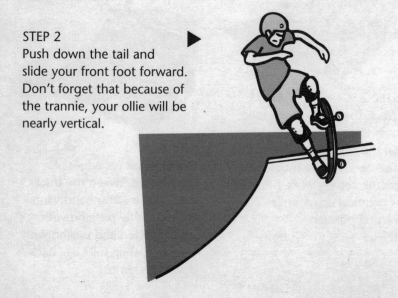

STEP 3
At the highest point of your ollie, grab the rail just behind your front foot with your leading hand.

STEP 4
As you descend from your air, release the deck just before you hit the ramp and ride down fakie. It's much safer to release the board a little late than too early.

New lines

Whenever you're at a park, always try to find new lines to skate. Watch other skaters and see if they've found a route you've never attempted.

85

Boneless wonder

If you want to catch some air, but aren't sure if you're ready to ollie off a ramp, try the boneless. To get extra height, you gently push your foot on the coping. Get in your boneless practice on a low mini-ramp or the shallow end of a bowl.

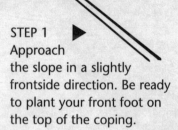

STEP 1 ▶
Approach the slope in a slightly frontside direction. Be ready to plant your front foot on the top of the coping.

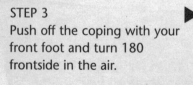

◀ **STEP 2**
Crouch down and grab the rail with your trailing hand, press down with your back foot to lift the nose, and take your front foot off the board and plant it on the coping – all at the same time!

STEP 3 ▶
Push off the coping with your front foot and turn 180 frontside in the air.

STEP 4
While still in the air, place your front foot back on the board and release your grip on the deck. ▶

STEP 5
Prepare to land with both legs bent. Then, look at your mates and say, "Sick or what?!" ▶

Fastplant

If you jump with your back foot rather than your front one, you're doing a fastplant. To pull off a fastplant, you'll need to do a little ollie at the top of the coping so that you can plant your back foot on the coping.

What a catch!

Now you've tasted air, it's time to get gnarly. The ollie stalefish may not sound like something you'd go near with a toy skateboard but, actually, moves don't come much radder. Pull off this mixture of ollie, back hand grab and 180, and you'll be so stoked you won't know what to do with yourself.

▲

STEP 1
Aim your board up a mini-ramp, ready to ollie off the top into a 180 turn.

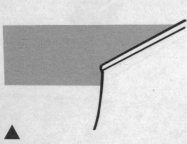

▲

STEP 2
As you ollie and start to turn, move your trailing hand behind your back leg towards the heel edge.

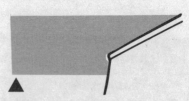

▲

STEP 3
Whilst turning in the air, bend your back leg and grab the deck with your trailing hand.

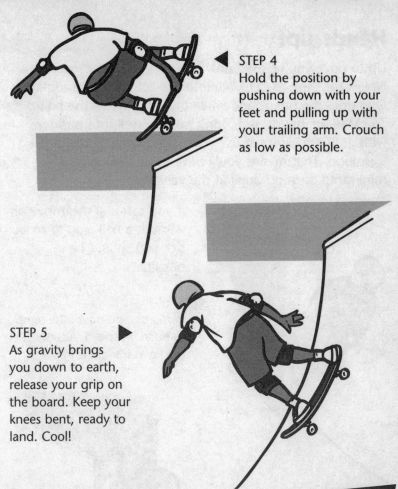

STEP 4
Hold the position by pushing down with your feet and pulling up with your trailing arm. Crouch as low as possible.

STEP 5
As gravity brings you down to earth, release your grip on the board. Keep your knees bent, ready to land. Cool!

Control counts

In any trick, it's not how massive the air is or whether you're going really fast that matters – it's how controlled and clean the move is that counts. But if you can do it really fast, really high and still be in control, you're doubly sick!

Hands up!

Up to now, you've used only one hand during moves. Now's the time to get both into the act for the handplant. One does the handstand while the other grabs the board. To make the handstand, don't pull yourself into position with your arm, instead use your speed coming out of the transition. That means you'll have to be sessioning a mini-ramp or good bowl at the very least.

If you can pull this move off without a bail, you're *soooo* sick you should be in hospital!

◀ STEP 1
Pump up and down the ramp to build up speed. Approach the lip at a slight angle.

STEP 2 ▶
Bend down as you near the coping, and grab the rail of the deck with your leading hand.

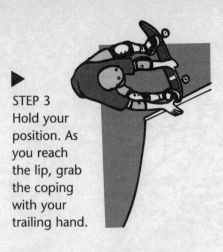

▶

STEP 3
Hold your
position. As
you reach
the lip, grab
the coping
with your
trailing hand.

STEP 4
When you're directly over the coping,
straighten your trailing arm to do the
handstand, and use your leading arm
to pull the board above you, right over
the coping.

▶

STEP 5 ▶
Remain in this one-armed
handstand position while
you turn
the board
through 90
degrees.
The board
will be
parallel to
the coping.

◀ STEP 6
Keep the turn going as you swing back down
again towards the ramp, release all grabs and
land smoothly on all four wheels.

Press play

A great way of learning new tricks or of sussing how to perfect old ones is by watching specialist skateboarding videos. These vids have great slow motion sequences, lots of easy-to-follow instructions and heaps of tips. You can play through the crucial stuff frame-by-frame to see just how the pros pull rad moves.

The videos can be quite expensive, so see if you can borrow them off friends or club together with mates to spread the cost. If you're not sure what to buy, check out the latest release video reviews in a skate mag or on the web. They'll tell you what each vid is about, how good it is and if it's worth the cash. You and your crew could also try hassling the local library to see if they could add skate videos to their lending list.

An American company, Four One One (411), produces what are generally recognised as the best skateboarding video magazines. They bring a new one out every couple of months, and their catalogue of videos covers everything from basic moves to pros at their most wicked.

Other videos will feature one particular aspect of skateboarding – such as slides, grinds or vert moves. So, if you want to concentrate on one area of your skating, get a vid that covers that move. A clued-up assistant at your skate shop should be able to recommend one.

Health warning

The skaters pulling cool moves on videos probably slammed ten times before they got it right. So don't expect to nail tricks first time. When in doubt – take it low and keep it slow.

Do it yourself

When you and your crew go to a comp or a pro demo, take a camcorder with you. Catch the sickest moves on tape and then play it back at home to work how to lick those slick tricks. Only two things to remember: get there early so you can get set up in a good position close to the action, and take the lens cap off!

Pro quote

"Taking skating photos is hard work, and more often than not, things don't go at all smoothly when you first start. Hence, stay with it."
Aaron Brown, pro skate photographer

9 On the meet

In a jam

Skateboarding, unlike football, rugby and basketball, isn't a team game – but that doesn't mean it's a lonely sport. On the contrary, skate jams, when riders get together for a meet, are always great fun.

Most jams are informal get-togethers organised by a few skaters who want to have a skate party. They are a great way to meet new faces and hook up with other skaters in your area. You'll hear about meets at your local park or see posters advertising them in skate shops.

If you are lucky, there will be a demo by some pro skaters. Pros know how frustrating learning new moves can be and most will be happy to help you work out how to pull off that elusive trick. But be patient – everybody wants to speak to the pros at jams!

Jams and competitions usually have a sticker toss. This is when stickers or other skate goodies are thrown to the scrambling crowd.

It's your party

If there aren't any events happening at your local park, why not organise one yourself? The owner of the park is usually more than willing to help, because skate events attract extra crowds and loads of free publicity.

you are invited to a skate Jam at the local park

DRESS iS SKATER COOL

Speak to your local skate shop – they may be willing to help you organise or advertise the event. Shops are usually keen on skate jams, because it gives them an opportunity to sell their merchandise.

It's also worth contacting the managers of some of the pro teams and see if they would be willing to send a team down to do a demo. If not, they'll probably send you some stickers or other stuff to give away at your jam. Contact addresses and telephone numbers for the pro teams can be found in skate magazines.

Don't forget to put up posters, and notify local papers at least three weeks in advance. If you're lucky, the newspaper might even send a photographer to catch the action.

Super stunts

At every meet, there is always someone who will try to pull an impressive trick, but he or she will have to go long way to match Tony Hawk.

One of the most successful pros the sport has seen, Tony has pulled just about every move that's ever been invented and has placed first in more comps than any other pro. And who will ever forget Tony's loop-the-loop round a massive circular pipe?

But when it comes to loopy, Danny Way takes the biscuit. He leapt out of a helicopter hovering above a vert ramp to record a 5.5 metre (18 feet) -high air – the biggest air ever documented. Is the man crazy? Way is way crazy!

Enter here

Most skate parks run competitions with sections for different age groups. Comps are great fun as long as you don't take them too seriously. To help cover the organiser's costs a competition entry fee is normally changed.

There are usually two contests at a comp – a street section and a vert section. In both of these, the competitors are given one or two minutes in which to show their stuff. A couple of minutes may seem like a short period, but it feels like an hour when everyone's watching you.

Pro quote

"As a judge you look for style, technical tricks and how someone is using the ramp or course. Riders can't just skate in straight lines."

Pete Dosset, judge and ex-pro

Some people zoom around covering every centimetre of the course or ramp, others concentrate on doing a couple of really rad tricks. There's no right or wrong way, so make your own choice.

Each of your runs is given a mark, but only the higher mark counts. The competitors with the three highest scores will bag skate gear as their prize. Bigger comps often award prize money, but these events also attract the pro skaters.

You're bound to be nervous when you enter a comp but don't worry, you're not the only one. Daewon Song, professional skateboard supremo, still gets nervous strutting his stuff in front of an audience. To counter the butterflies, Daewon focuses on the basic line, knowing that if he gets that right, the technical moves will fit in naturally.

Deck bangers

Show your appreciation for sick moves at comps by banging your deck on the ramp or ground.

No park?

Not everyone is lucky enough to have a skate park nearby, but it is possible to persuade your local council to build one. All it takes, as Will Barraclough from Crawley in the United Kingdom found out, is persistence, persistence and more persistence!

Every year for six years, Will hassled his local council. He kept up a constant barrage of proposals that included suggestions for park designers and rough costings. The turning point came when Will got a summer job in the local highways department. He used contacts he made there to increase the pressure he was already putting on the council, and a year later the park was finished. Result!

Will's tips

- Work out a financial proposal to prove to those in the council that a skate park is affordable.
- Get parents, teachers, community officers, the police, guide and scout leaders, shop-keepers, and anyone else you can think of, on your side. Do this with leaflets, posters, a petition or by calling a meeting in a local hall.
- Organise a letter-writing campaign to councillors, pointing out the benefits of a skate park.
- Get the local press interested by sending them reports and photographs about your campaign.
- Organise a publicity stunt that will focus attention on the need for a skate park. You and your crew could give a display of your ace skate skills.
- Don't give up!

If there seems to be nothing you can do to persuade the council to build a skate park, you may be able to entice local entrepreneurs to help. Try appealing in local newspapers for financial support. If the park makes sound business sense, these people may build and operate the park, or they may be able to work in partnership with the council. In the end, it doesn't matter who builds and manages the park, as long as it's built.

So you want to be a pro?

I have a dream ...

So, you want to be a ...
SKATEBOARDER?!!

CAREERS OFFICER

Anyone who's ever skated has thought about being a pro. Imagine: you spend your time doing your favourite pastime, you are given all the equipment and clothes you need, and, what's more, you get paid for it. It seems like skate heaven. But, of course, the reality is a little different.

There are different levels of professional skating – from those just starting out to those who earn big money. It is only a handful though who make it all the way to the top.

The first step in any pro's skateboarding career is finding or being found by a sponsor. A sponsor is usually a manufacturer in the skate industry who is willing to give a skater their products for free on the understanding that the skater is seen using them. This means that the skater has to be very good at promoting and representing the brand at comps, meets and in the media.

So you want to be a pro?

The sponsors choose their skaters very carefully. They don't want someone who won't enter comps, won't try out new tricks or isn't really interested in turning others onto the greatest sport around. What they really want is a cool, up-and-coming skater who'll work hard at perfecting their ride and moves, come up with ideas for new stunts and get out there – no matter what – among the grommets to enthuse about skating and the manufacturer's equipment. You see, when you become a professional, skateboarding becomes much like any other job (only radder!).

Words from the wise guys

Pros Tony Hawk and Andy MacDonald are two of the world's greatest skaters but it wasn't talent alone that got them to the top – it took a lot of hard work, too.

Tony remembers one move, the kickflip 540, that he couldn't nail. "It was a joke, I just couldn't work it out," he recalls. "It took me a whole month, practising it every day, before I came close. My first attempts were insanely disgusting, almost spinning out! I eventually got the hang of it, but it took time."

Andy, too, found that he had to work at perfecting moves. "I used to keep a list of all the tricks I wanted to do," he says. "When I was younger, I never went to the ramp just to muck around. I would skate for the first 30 minutes and then spend the rest of the time – all day if possible – working on my moves. It paid off."

Dave Evans, an Australian pro skater has this to add: "Skateboarding teaches you self-discipline. You learn that you've got to stick at something until you've nailed it. You can apply this self-discipline to achieving anything in life."

Getting sponsored

If you think you're good enough, you could try contacting your local skate shop and asking if they would sponsor you. But, the chances are, if you are that good, someone will have already picked you up. The more normal route is through amateur competitions.

Another way of attracting attention is to get your picture in a skate mag. Magazines like good quality photos of rad moves, preferably taken in new and unusual spots.

If you have a friend who is into photography, try to set up a shoot. Send the results off to your favourite mag, with short notes explaining what is happening in each photo. If any pictures are printed, don't forget to keep a copy of the magazine so that you can show it to possible sponsors. That one story could just make the difference!

The sponsors

Jon Robson of Unabomber Skateboards in the United Kingdom, currently sponsors seven amateur riders. An amateur rider is someone who does not get paid any sort of wage. Jon gives his riders a small package of boards every month. This means that the rider has enough boards for his or her own needs; the rest they can sell. Some companies don't like riders doing this, but everybody has to make a living. And, as Jon adds, "for most amateur riders it's a pretty meagre living."

Pro Chad Knight found his sponsor by sending videos of his skating to just about every skate company around. One manufacturer was so impressed that he added Chad to the team. Chad's sound advice to any would-be professionals is: "Persistence – that's what it's all about."

Once you are sponsored, the next step is to get picked up by a pro team. Most manufacturers have a skate team that performs demos and enters comps. The team gets to travel a lot, often abroad, but it does mean they are constantly in demand and always on the go.

Pro quote

"You've got to do all the things that come with the job. Going out and doing demos, going to all the contests and keeping your sponsors happy. It can get a bit stressful."

Rune Glifberg, pro skateboarder

Once you become a pro, you will also get paid on top of the equipment package. The size of the cheque depends on the company and how respected you are within the skate community.

Pro quote

"I had two knee injuries, right after each other and couldn't skate for months. But I still had to be in the public eye for my sponsors. That's what being a pro means."

Paul Sharpe, pro skateboarder

The professional scene is improving all the time in Europe, Australia and South Africa – but, at present, a skater who's looking for big competitions and big bucks has little choice apart from trying his or her luck in America. In the States, the skateboard business is big business!

Pro quote

"In Britain, professional skating is not worth a lot of money — just enough to survive on. But in the United States it's totally different."

Paul Shier, pro skateboarder

Pro-skater Bob Burnquist left his native Brazil in South America to try and make it in the United States. "When I was a pro in Brazil, I wasn't making enough money to keep up with new gear so that I could progress, let alone eat!" recalls Bob. Now, he regularly places in comps where the top prize money is in the thousands.

"Being a great skater," explains Bob, "takes a lot of focus, dedication and confidence. All I do now, is skate, skate, skate." Fellow professional Danny Way agrees: "You can really tell when someone has been skating hard. Consistency pays off."

Signature boards

The really top pros have a 'signature' board or shoe. Working alongside a manufacturer, the pro will help to design a board or shoe, and will then be paid a percentage of the price for every one that is sold. If the 'signature' product is successful, those percentages can add up to good money. Unfortunately, there are not many pro skaters who have been so fortunate.

Pro quote

"Without skateboarding, I wouldn't have had this great life of fun, travelling, meeting cool people, and money with no nine-to-five job. The best advice is keep skating and have fun."
Mike Carroll, pro skateboarder

While many of us would love to be a pro, very few will make it. Worldwide there is probably only one pro for every 60,000 skaters. That means there are vast numbers of skateboarders out there who are doing it for only one reason – because they love it.

Whether it's the buzz from pulling an ollie or the adrenaline rush from nailing a rail slide, the only things skaters need to enjoy themselves are some set-ups and some concrete. Waves? Surfboards? Ha, who needs 'em?

So, go on, take your board – thrash it, smash it, trash it! But, above all, enjoy it.

Pro quote

"Skateboarding is an expression of a individual's style and who they are. Enjoy skateboarding, knowing there are no limits to what you can achieve. I'm stoked to be a part of the people and scene of skateboarding."
Chad J Bartie, pro skateboarder

109

Skate parks and shops

This small selection of parks and shops gives you a starting point if you're looking for new thrills or equipment. Contact these places during their quiet times – they'll appreciate it and be able to spend more time helping you. Telephone numbers have been included wherever possible.

UNITED KINGDOM
Skate parks
Aberdeen: Stoneywood Skate Park (01224) 626996
Bristol: Skate and Ride (0117) 907 9995
Glasgow: Livingston Statepark
Hull: Rock City (01482) 223030
London: Harrow Skate Park (020) 8863 9371
London: Romford Skate Park (01708) 474429
Manchester: Bones SK8 Park (0161) 480 8118
Northampton: Radlands (01604) 702060

Shops
Birmingham: Boardwise (0121) 212 2500
Bournemouth: The Consortium (01202) 318 473
Bristol: Fifty Fifty (0117) 929 4322
Coventry: Kong (024) 7652 0972
Edinburgh: Boardwise (0131) 229 5887
Glasgow: Clan (0141) 339 6523
London: Slam City Skates (020) 7240 0928
Nottingham: Rollersnakes (01332) 200012
Port Rush: Woodies (01265) 823273
Southampton: Off Beat Sorts (01703) 330 600

AUSTRALIA

Skate parks

Adelaide, SA: Ridge Park, (free)

Caloundra, Qld: Cooparoo
Skatepark (07) 3225 6757

Canberra, ACT: Bellconnenn
Skate Park

Cranbourne, Vic: Skate Shed
(03) 5996 6811

Fitzroy, Vic: Fitzroy Bowl (free)

Gold Coast, Qld: Pizzey Park

Manly, NSW: Keirle Park (free)

Perth, WA: Vert X Skate Park (09) 9524 3882

Penrith, NSW: Vert X Skate Park (047) 33 0004

Southport, Qld: Skateworld (07) 5591 5733

Sydney: Skate Shed (02) 9651 4354

Taren Point, NSW: Vert X (02) 9524 1675

Tuggerah, NSW: Level 2 Indoor Skate Park (02) 4352 2374

Werribee, Vic: Blades Indoor Skate Park

Shops

Adelaide, SA: Skateboard World (08) 8377 3393

Bendigo, Vic: Wooz (03) 5441 6257

Brisbane, Qld: Skate Biz (07) 3220 0157

Burwood, NSW: Skateboard World (02) 9744 2785

Canberra, ACT: Ollie-on Skateboards (02) 625 1698

Cronulla, NSW: Sheridan's (02) 9523 5675

Claremont WA: Bladeskate (09) 9246 9200

Fremantle, WA: Momentum Skate Shop (09) 9430 4082

Homebush, NSW: Room 101 (02) 9763 1555

Melbourne, Vic: PSC (03) 9783 3811

Surry Hills, NSW: Shut up and Skate (02) 9360 3113

Skate parks and shops

SOUTH AFRICA
The skate scene in South Africa is based around
Johannesburg. In other towns, contact surf shops for
more information.

Skate parks
Johannesburg: Boogaloos Skatepark, (011) 622 6185
Johannesburg: Look Ahead Skatepark (011) 793 6613
Natal: Rox Skatepark (031) 337 4069
Pretoria: Boogaloos Skatepark (012) 348 0670

Shops
Cape Town: Corner Surf Shop
(021) 788 1191
Durban: Board Sailing
(031) 337 4069
East London: Billabong
(0423) 931 210
Johannesburg: Boogaloos
(011) 823 4312
Port Elizabeth: Beach Break
(041) 554 303

Read all about it!

Skateboarding magazines are a great way of keeping in touch with what's happening locally, nationally and even internationally. They'll give you the latest on comps, special events, as well lots of features brimming with cool pics. Just as useful when you're looking for equipment, are the advertisements.

UNITED KINGDOM
'Sidewalk Surfer': Permanent Publishing, 1 Sturt Street, Abingdon, Oxford OX14 3JF

AUSTRALIA
'Australian Skateboarding':
PO Box 746, Darlinghurst,
NSW 2010
'Slam': PO Box 823,
Burleigh Heads, Qld 4220

SOUTH AFRICA
'Blunt': Zig Zag Publications,
PO Box 47463, Greyville,
Durban 4023

UNITED STATES
You can pick up copies of the latest issues of State-side mags like 'Big Brother', 'Thrasher', 'Slap' and 'Transworld Skateboarding' from your local skate shop.

Cyberskate

Check out these Internet sites for the latest and hottest skateboard news and gossip. More and more sites are appearing every day, so cruise as often as you can. All you have to do is type in 'Skateboarding' and the world becomes one big skate park.

http://www.skateboard.co.uk/
> British site with UK skate news, events and interviews.

http://www.ram.net.au/users/global/
> Australian site with what's happening where and when Down Under.

http://www.colony.dircon.co.uk/
> Comprehensive online resource for British skaters.

http://www.webtrax.com/skate/
> Well-organised American skateboarding site with great links to other skate sites across the world wide web.

Glossary

180	A 180 degree turn (said 'one-eighty')
180 ollie	Move combining ollie and kickturn
360	A 360 degree turn (said 'three-sixty')
5-0	Grinding with the rear truck (said 'five-o')
50-50	Grinding with both trucks (said 'fifty-fifty')
Acid drop	Skating off the end of an object
Air trick	Skater leaves the ground, often off a ramp
Axle stall	Move where the board rests on trucks on the lip of a ramp
Backside	Any move in the direction your toes point
Bail	Jumping off your board when a trick goes wrong
Baseplate	Attaches truck to deck
Blunt	Landing with the tail on the edge of an object and the rear wheel on top of the object. The nose will be near vertical
Boardslide	Sliding on a rail or similar on the middle of your board, with the trucks hanging either side of the rail
Boned	Mid-air trick where the board is pushed out in front
Boneless	Taking off by using the front foot to push off the ground, and grabbing the side of the board
Bowl	Sunken concrete or wooden area found in a skate park

Glossary

Bushings	Thick pieces of rubber within the truck that help steering
Concave	Curve on deck that helps a rider balance
Coping	Metal piping running along top of a ramp
Crooked grind	Grinding on the front truck with the board not over the object
Deck	Skateboard's wooden platform
Delam	When the plywood layers of the board's deck separate
Disaster	Rear wheels on top of an object, deck on edge of it, with front wheels hanging off
Drop in	Move used to enter ramp from platform
Fakie	Travelling backwards
Fastplant	Boneless off back foot
Feeble grind	Grinding with the rear truck while the front truck hangs over the toe edge of the object without touching it
Frontside	Moves in the direction your heels face
Fun box	A platform with four banked sides used on street courses
Gnarly	Fast and exciting
Goofy foot	Skating with your left foot at the back
Grab	Using your hand to hold the board during a move
Grind	Moving along an object on your trucks
Griptape	Sandpaper-type material stuck to the top of the deck that helps skater stay on board

Grommet	A skateboarder who's a learner
Handplant	A handstand
Hanger	Holds axle on which wheels turn
Heelflip	Spinning the board round with the front foot heel while in the air
Jam	Meeting of skateboarders for a skate session
K-grind	See Crooked grind
Kickfilp	Spinning the board with a kicking motion, while in the air
Kicktail	Curved tail at the back of the skateboard
Kickturn	Turning on the rear wheels with the front wheels off the ground
Kingpin	Bolt that holds the truck to the baseplate
Line	Route skateboarder takes over obstacles or course
Lip	Top edge of ramp or bowl
Liptrick	Move performed on the lip of a ramp
Manual	A wheelie – riding on just the back wheels
Mini-ramp	U-shaped ramp (6 feet) high
Nollie	An ollie performed from the nose
Nose	Front of the board
Nosegrab	Grabbing the front of the board with the leading hand
Nosegrind	Grinding on the leading truck
Noseslide	Sliding the nose over an object with the rest of the board hanging off object

Glossary

Obstacle	Object that can be used to pull a trick on
Ollie	Jumping with your board without using your hands or a ramp
Ollie stalefish	A turn in the air, whilst holding the board with rear hand behind the back leg
Ollie to axle	Ollie, then landing on trucks on the edge of an object
Phat	Trick performed really 'big' or over a long distance (said 'fat').
Pool	Another term for bowl
Popping	Action of pushing on the kicktail that enables an ollie
Pop shove-it	Board turning 180 degrees horizontally in the air
Pro	Professional skateboarder
Pro board	A deck sold under the name of a pro skater
Pumping	Using the body's momentum to rise up a transition
Rad	Brilliant or spectacular
Rails	Underside edges of the board
Regular foot	Skating with your right foot at the back
Rock	Position where front wheels and middle of board rest on top of ramp
Rock fakie	Rolling up ramp into rock position before rolling backwards

Rock 'n' roll	A move where you ride to the top of a ramp, push the front truck over the lip, stop, then turn and roll back down
Set-up	Skateboard, and also how you choose to put together the different parts of a board
Shove-it	Turning the board through 180 degrees while in the air
Shred	See Thrash
Sick	Particularly impressive move or trick
Sketchy	Only just landing a trick, and also risky when referring to a sketchy skate spot
Slalom	Quick series of turns in and out of cones or bollards
Slam	Falling off your board
Slick	Plastic layer fitted to the bottom of deck to aid sliding
Slide	Trick where the board slides along an object
Smithgrind	Grinding with the rear truck, while the front truck runs along the side of the object
Snake	Someone who pushes into a queue
Spacer	Piece of metal that separates wheel bearings to ensure smooth running
Spine	Ridge produced when two ramps are placed back-to back
Spot	Area suitable for skating
Stance	How you stand on the board, either regular or goofy
Stick	Another word for a skateboard
Stoked	Extremely pleased
Street	A style of skating that is suited to pavements, streets and other public areas. Also, a section of competitions held on a street-style course

Glossary

Switch stance	Performing tricks in the stance that's not your natural stance
Tail	Rear of the board
Tail grab	Grabbing the rear of the board
Tail slide	Sliding the tail over an object with the rest of the board hanging off the object
Tail stall	Resting on coping on the tail only
Thrash	To wear down your board through skating
Tic-tac	Moving forward through a series of small kickturns
Toss	A free-for-all at competitions when stickers and skate goodies are thrown to the crowd
Trannie or transition	The part of a ramp or bank that curves upwards
Truck	Metal hanger and axle that fixes the wheels to the deck
Vert	Large U-shaped ramp. Also, a section of competitions held on a vert ramp
Wallride	Skating on a vertical wall
Wood	Deck with painted graphics and no slick

Index

Index

super.activ

All you need to know

0 340 773294	Acting	£3.99	☐
0 340 764686	Athletics	£3.99	☐
0 340 791578	Basketball	£3.99	☐
0 340 791535	Cartooning	£3.99	☐
0 340 791624	Chess	£3.99	☐
0 340 791586	Computers Unlimited	£3.99	☐
0 340 79156X	Cricket	£3.99	☐
0 340 791594	Drawing	£3.99	☐
0 340 791632	Film-making	£3.99	☐
0 340 791675	Fishing	£3.99	☐
0 340 791519	Football	£3.99	☐
0 340 76466X	Golf	£3.99	☐
0 340 778970	Gymnastics	£3.99	☐
0 340 791527	In-line Skating	£3.99	☐
0 340 749504	Karate	£3.99	☐
0 340 791640	The Internet	£3.99	☐
0 340 791683	Memory Workout	£3.99	☐
0 340 736283	Pop Music	£3.99	☐
0 340 791551	Riding	£3.99	☐
0 340 791659	Rugby	£3.99	☐
0 340 791608	Skateboarding	£3.99	☐
0 340 791667	Snowboarding	£3.99	☐
0 340 791616	Swimming	£3.99	☐
0 340 764465	Tennis	£3.99	☐
0 340 773332	Writing	£3.99	☐
0 340 791543	Your Own Website	£3.99	☐

Turn the page to find out how to order these books.

ORDER FORM

Books in the super.activ series are available at your local bookshop, or can be ordered direct from the publisher. A complete list of titles is given on the previous page. Just tick the titles you would like and complete the details below. Prices and availability are subject to change without prior notice.

Please enclose a cheque or postal order made payable to Bookpoint Ltd, and send to: Hodder Children's Books, Cash Sales Dept, Bookpoint, 39 Milton Park, Abingdon, Oxon OX14 4TD. Email address: orders@bookpoint.co.uk.

If you would prefer to pay by credit card, our call centre team would be delighted to take your order by telephone. Our direct line is 01235 400414 (lines open 9.00 am – 6.00 pm, Monday to Saturday; 24-hour message answering service). Alternatively you can send a fax on 01235 400454.

Title .... First name .... Surname ....

Address ....

....

....

Daytime tel .... Postcode.....................................

If you would prefer to post a credit card order, please complete the following.

Please debit my Visa/Access/Diner's Card/American Express (delete as applicable) card number:

Signature ....Expiry Date ....

If you would NOT like to receive further information on our products, please tick ☐ .